POSITIVES

Also by Thom Gunn

*

VERSES BY
THOM GUNN

POSITIVES

PHOTOGRAPHS BY
ANDER GUNN

THE UNIVERSITY OF CHICAGO PRESS

The University of Chicago Press, Chicago 60637
Faber and Faber Limited, London, W.C.1, England

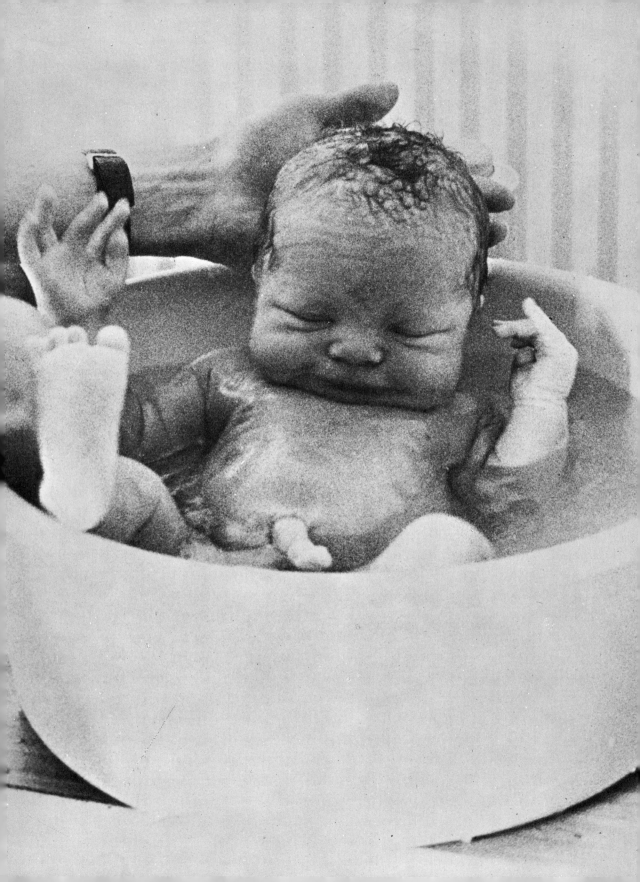

She has been a germ, a fish,
and an animal; even now
she is almost without hair
or sex. But the body
is feeling its way
                    feeling:
the minute hands grip, the big
baldish head beams, the feet
press out in the strange element

there is a perception of
warm water, warm, but cooling

The body blunders forward
into the next second, in
its awkward bold half-aware
fashion, and getting there too
— doing things for the first time.

Precarious exploration
from coast to interior:
by which a workable route is
opened, for the later transport
of lathes, heavy crosses and
crates through the undergrowth.

Meanwhile, before the next push,
a triumph, a triumph.

But childhood takes a long time.

Something is feeding on you,
and it is what you feed on.
The source of your strength guts you.

Cars pass by on the street,
and as you feel a loose tooth, in
pleasurable pain, you think
'there is pleasure in reaching
a painful conclusion
with a tooth or with a thought.'

'Drink Me'
'Eat Me'
and you grew or shrank.
Here you have to wait.

In a bus it is nice to ride on top because it looks like running people over.

In watchful community
when we ought to be at school

sheltering by the warehouse
we stand, smelling
creosote, and the musty
rot of wood from floorboards
where sacks have lain, for
years, huddled together.

That is behind us, but
in front we hear the
plop of rain, and
while we stand
our bodies are increasing
in secret society.

He rides up and down, and around:
all things are means to wheely ends.
All things radiate from the spokes under
that hard structure of bars crossing
precisely and usefully. But another
leans against an iron fence, grown
older, and dreams of cars.

and they start to cross the road,
life swelling in them, but still
contained — aware of their health,
and cherishing their containment

swelling buds
compact segmented buds
bees will come to them
and pollen will encrust
will weigh the treading of
those black hairy legs
till the bees are so heavy
that they seem drunk, uncertain
wavering
in heavy flight from the flowers

Youth is power. He knows it,
a rough young animal, but
an animal that can smile.

He growls playfully, shaking
dew from the bushes
as he pokes his way through them
into the world beyond,
at ease in his power. For
can there be limits?

He makes, now,
a fine gesture, inviting
experience to try him.

She rests on and in
the laugh with her whole body, like
an expert swimmer who
lies back in the water
playing relaxed with
her full uncrippled strength
in a sort of hearty surprise

or the laugh is like a prelude:
the ripples go outward
over cool water, losing
force, but continue
to be born at the centre, wrinkling
the water around it

𝄞 The music starts ‖ tentative
nobody notices it
they go on drinking, talking,
absorbed in ‖ the music starts
they do hear behind and
at the edges of themselves how
something is encroaching, how
something is ‖ it is a song
about life by the Mersey
they begin to recognise
that ‖ the music has started

PETE

Mackie's indubitably
back in town. After work
he is covered with dry mud,
his boots dead stumps, his
fingers feeling like things
in their casts of yellow clay.

But those clamps for a spade
turn, at evening,
by plastic flowers grown
from no clay, to delicate
and precise instruments.

two mirrors
for the self-regarding rider
the learner
tentative but with increasing
momentum
he moves in on the world which he
examines
by a battery of headlights
the scooter
he rides is named after himself
the seat is
like an obedient leopard
a damp wind
forced from the standing air in front
absorbs him
he catches sight of his own face
and does not
know it against the new landscape

It is a lament, and then
it is not. For the clear voice
has discovered, under the opaque
level, the bubbling source
of both joy and lamentation:
feeling is the thrust in
the transparent knot, and is
the knot itself, and is
the ripples which course out from that
centre, ridged with strength.

an impetus: its roar, its music
mastering and yet
mastered by the body

The external world becomes
abstract, a wind
on water, or on the road

it resists, but resistance
defines the impetus,
of which the hard centre
is a gentleness
projected at great speed

She can't help it, can't
help it. To find it is
evening among the Dodgems,
is luck, an overflowing
like tears, uncontrollable:

arc-lamps through the soft dusk,
boys and girls dawdling
over grass and chocolate wrappers.

Something pulses in her, warm,
rapid, and regular, with a
music she can almost hear

and to this music she dances
the dance of her luck.

She trembles slightly: her flesh
feels hardly strong enough
for the weight of white lace
which seems to overwhelm her

in her shy smile
choice meets delight
which is fair and fragile

She is giving herself
in trust so complete, so
vulnerable to
the attack of happiness
that you catch your breath
at the risk

      yet waiting
she bears the lace like
her own tender handmaiden
how clear, how soft, and how firm

The responsibilities
of marriage follow, of course:

Tesco, Woolworth, and
Archie's

      you will get home
and I will give you a big
tea on our own table.

In a family, there is
a sense of many doing
many things, all different,
absorbed, in different rooms.

You grow accustomed to this:
the Rostovs have different
personalities, you say. Then
suddenly a door opens

and all the Rostov children
come out together, doing
the same thing in the same way.

No music in this boozer.
She says she's with her
mother, though my
theory is it's a fellow.

I doze into a twilight,
a dry foul taste in my mouth,
nodding on the brown cracked
American leather of the sofa.

SYON HOUSE

a distant sound of water,
dew on blackberry bushes
globing the thorns, glossing
the mauve, slightly whiskered
segments of unripe berries

but there is a mystery: strange
forms push in from outside;
I am oppressed by a sense of columns.
I push back, but their pressure
is continual because
they have no mind or feeling
to vacillate

LEBENSRAUM

Life should be a humane
undertaking. I know. I
undertook it.

            Yet have found
that in my every move
I prevent someone
from stepping where I step.

So I must run into the open,
alone, to wait on the
untrodden acres of snow
among black trunks, till
the bacillus of despair is
rendered harmless:
isolated and frozen over.

Like a cliff, Marble
Arch Odeon stood
black above the traffic.

It is gone, more
than gone, a hollow
where the encrusted cliff was.

No commissionaires now.
A donkey jacket
swings on a rail.

There is a clear
drop: and in the puddled
mud at the bottom

distant men in caps
move about the uneven
space, below the mixer's

belly, setting bars
in concrete, their own bulk
submerged in sunlight.

We didn't do up this pub,
though we painted the pipes round
the walls gold, and we put up
little chandeliers

but it is
still divided with ornate
scrolled wood, there are still
snob-screens in a twinkling row.
There were big glass mirrors
till the protection boys came
and broke them, for a warning.

About her routine, she
moves from smells of hops and
malt to medicinal or
fruity smells, which
haunt the polished wood,
each in its place

not like them redecorated
pubs down Chelsea.

He raises the pick, point against
the sky, his own weight divided
fairly between his legs,
right hand lower to guide and
steady the handle, left hand
higher to bear the pick down
on the inanimate rubble
which must be broken, levelled
by unskilled labour — But there is
skill in getting the proper
stance — Through an arc the point
falls as force, the human
behind it in control
tiring, but tiring slowly

Money is a form of dirt
to be shovelled around. Yet
for clients and subordinates
your expression must appear
weighty, for dirt has weight.
Clients and subordinates
too, perceive the context
of weightiness, they even
start to put on weight, and
the resemblance between all of us
is deepened by the crowning
weight of our bowlers, from
which weight seeps so potently that
sometimes we have to take them off.

The rubble rises in smoke.
One would, perhaps, prefer an
air pure and open, tempered only
by the smell of grass or the sea.
But the smoke is everywhere, is
unescapable, is an inhabited
confusion, bitter-smelling, laden
with foul particles and soft
light blobs of carbon like
black snowflakes. People
fumble toward each other through
the greasy obscurity. On the downs
one would be merely alone.

At times, on the edge of smoke
— what is it?
                    Smack smack
grunting
fumbling toward each other
half-glimpsed (I want to
get you out of the WAY)
words will not do, it has
to be got from the blood
— the music has come back
but distorted, uncontrolled:
impulse as excreta
half-glimpsed (I want to
get myself out of the WAY)

The liver and onions is off,
so is golden sponge pud. So,
it appears, are the customers.

You can tire of the town,
and the variety of the pavements
being endless, itself may need
varying. But with what?

I have closed my brief-case, dropped my
pick, stopped serving pints, thrown down the
broom, finished fighting: it is the tea-
break:

> *When God bade labour for our burden, He*
> *Relented slightly at the end,*
> *And granted respite twice a day, for tea.*
> *O Teapot, heavenly maid, descend.*

Make it strong, Jonesy
that's how I like it, strong
with plenty of sugar in it

You have no idea what a
hard life a rich person leads.

What with servants and jewels,
and having to go to Harrods
every day so as to
purchase a big article
and help use up the imports.

It's quite a relief sometimes
to sit down for a while with
an espresso and a tiny slice
of expensive cake.

You have no idea, either,
how hard it is
seeming to lead such a life.

The pigeon lifts, a few feet
from the ground, its wings outspread,
its pink claws clutched on themselves
like a baby's featured hands:
the span of wing flutters.

He is no young pigeon, he
has ceased fluttering, an old
man with a face like some gnarled
shiny section of black wood.
He sweeps rubble all day
off the streets, leavings
of other men his takings. The pigeon
flutters, the female cowers
in fear and delight. The sweeper,
his broom reversed in the gutter,
watches the girl, not with hope
or even much desire,
but with the care of a man
cataloguing an authentic
treasure in the quiet
collection of his mind.

The memoirs of the body
are inscribed on it: they make
an ambiguous story
because you can read
the lines two ways: as
the ability to resist
annihilation, or as the small
but constant losses endured

but between the lines
life itself! you can read
the plump puckers
                    while
the sentences cross and recross

(Please destroy in
the event of death.)

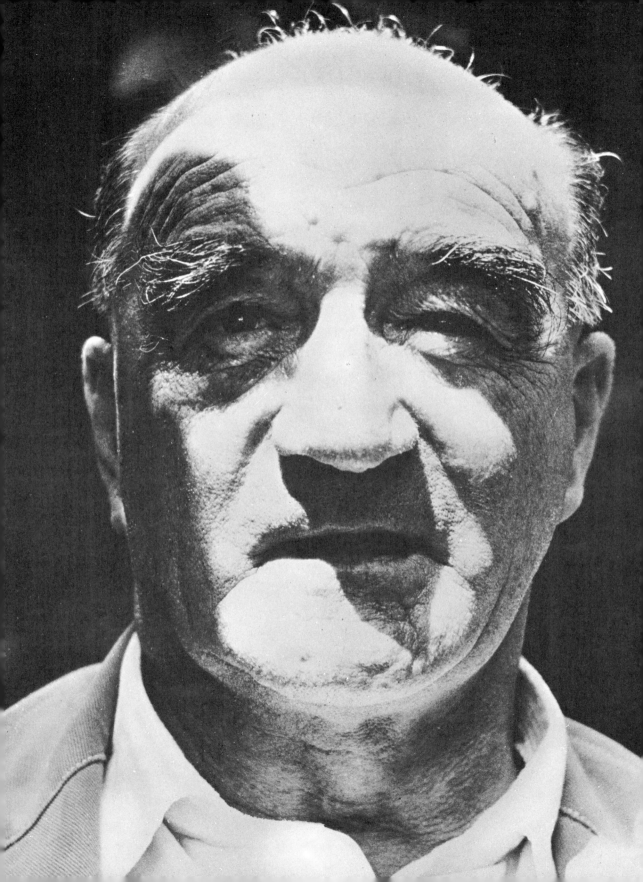

He feels a breeze rise from
the Thames, as far off
as Rotherhithe, in
intimate contact with
water, slimy hulls,
dark wood greenish
at waterline — touching
then leaving what it
lightly touches; he
goes on talking, and this is
the life of wind on water.

It is stone: and if ripples
touch the base of its arches,
he cannot feel them, cannot
feel more than the flat
stone of the bridge, and his bundle.

It is not a symbolic
bridge but a real bridge;
nor is the bundle
a symbol. The wind
is cold, stone
hard, and Salvation Army
tea not sweet enough.

The mould from baked beans that
even she can't eat edges
onto the damp sticks, netting,
bones, leaves, slabs
of rust, felt, feathers,

all disintegrating to
an infected compost.

The infection in it is slow,
slight, deep, and it has certain needs,
for see, it responds to warmth.

Outside the abandoned house
where she slept on old papers
she stirs in the sun.

Poking around the rubbish,
she can't find what she wants.

Near Maidstone once, hop-picking
with the four babies and Tom,
she worked all day along the green
alleys, among the bins,
in the dim leafy light of
the overhanging vines.

In the village, shopkeepers
put cages on their counters
to prevent snatching. But Tom
took something! What was it?

All in the rubbish heap now,
some rotting, most clean vanished.

Something approaches, about
which she has heard a good deal.
Her deaf ears have caught it, like
a silence in the wainscot
by her head. Her flesh has felt
a chill in her feet, a draught
in her groin. She has watched it
like moonlight on the frayed wood
stealing toward her
floorboard by floorboard. Will it hurt?

Let it come, it is
the terror of full repose,
and so no terror.